Because You Were Mine

Because You Were Mine

Poems | Brionne Janae

Published in 2023 by
Haymarket Books
P.O. Box 180165
Chicago, IL 60618
773-583-7884
www.haymarketbooks.org
info@haymarketbooks.org

ISBN: 978-1-64259-912-1

Distributed to the trade in the US through Consortium Book Sales and
Distribution (www.cbsd.com) and internationally through Ingram Publisher
Services International (www.ingramcontent.com).

This book was published with the generous support of Lannan Foundation,
Wallace Action Fund, and the Marguerite Casey Foundation.

Special discounts are available for bulk purchases by organizations and
institutions. Please email info@haymarketbooks.org for more information.

Cover design by Brett Neiman. Cover photograph is "Delores, Melrose
Plantation, Louisiana" by Carlotta Corpron. © 1988 Amon Carter Museum of
American Art.

Printed in Canada by union labor. Ⓤ

Library of Congress Cataloging-in-Publication data is available.

10 9 8 7 6 5 4 3 2 1

TELL THE TRUTH AND SHAME THE DEVIL
-ANONYMOUS

·

WITH GRATITUDE TO ALL WHO LOVED
AND HELD ME ALONG THE WAY.

CONTENTS

Against Confessional

you are not my god
I owe you no debt
nor gratitude
will gift
no object
cut and bleed
no sacrifice
in your name
I offer only
my voice
that it catch
in your throat
drag you in the rooms
you dare not enter
yet fill and fill
I offer you
your stink
your rot
your festering wound
I bring no salve
no balm
nor rag to bite
and silence the scream
charging up
from your diaphragm
I offer you
your scream
your voice
your tremble and terror
I carry only a mirror
held at the right angle
that you may see
and see all

I.

"Want and Love Are Not the Same Word"
after Nicole Homer

we used to sing *I need you to survive*
in church sunday mornings

the pastor would say *turn to your neighbor*
and we'd make eyes with strangers before god

and sing in the oversized congregation
where the youth came straight from the club

to the altar a sweater or shawl covering the skin
they'd let loose the night before

trying to catch a lover with the shine
of their shea butter-anointed flesh

need is not the same as want or love
but perhaps it is more honest

more insistent on our frailty our   humanness
personally I can't stand to be so exposed

if I acknowledge my soft human body
and all the ways it aches to be held

what happens when I still sit lonely
with no one to touch me and say *you are real*

somedays I'd rather die than admit my need
a flaw I'd best   not take to my grave

though I guess we all must carry something at the end

Nothing More Isolating Than a Body

acutely the lines come down around us
we each trapped in our own peculiar cells
unknowable one to the other
we spend all our lives learning to read
the pinch and crinkle of the skin
the limbs gesture   heads every particular angle
we may as well be divining stars
even without gods we beg manna and milk
to be told where to go   what to do
and how to bear the yoke of our bewilderment
please mother we say *tell me what you mean*

I Called It Grace

it's not what I remember but rather the blank spaces
that billow up like wind thrashing the trees

the moments between the first frenzied steps in flight
and the chill of a wall at my back

the not knowing what comes after
but knowing my mother was after me

on good days I call this absence
this blank space in the memory grace

imagine my mind like a photo album
pulled from the ash of a fire

know the heat blackened image is mine
not from what I can piece together through soot

but because the collapsed frame around it is home
here's one where I lie   face down on my mother's lap

in the apartment she and my father found
behind the Kmart by the freeway

the complex had a playground in the center
where a little blond boy called me nigger

I can still remember walking the path back home
to ask what the word meant

but not what happens next with my mother
was she about to strike or rub my back

she rarely touched me

and I was always so afraid

I don't know when the sound
of my name on her lips

became like the slow pull
of a knife tip down my spine

or rather the breathlessness
of the wind sucked out of me

but it is now was then too
when I bent my preschool body at the waste

and watched the tint of my mother's shadow
move between my feet

she swings
I run

I can remember my fear of the ladder
up to the bunk bed I never slept in

but not how in that panting moment
and through the darkness of the room

I got up there
I can see myself tucked

into a ball on the unused comforter
my back pressed against the wall

feet pulled into my body to keep
my mother from snatching me down

can still see the triangle of light at the door

feel the sweat of knowing

my mother was after me
but nothing else

nothing else at all

too long perhaps
I called *this* grace and love

the will of the mind to forget
what the body will always remember

FOR DEVONTE HART

I imagine your ghost as thin
and dark as your body clasped
around the armor of the officer who
in another two seconds might have peppered
your flesh with bullets   charged
your form with the sharp sting of voltage
lifted his arms and squeezed
the life from your lungs
either way you are lifeless now
and I cannot stop seeing you
reaching from harm to harm
tears cutting a path down
around your nose and cheek
as if a stream
on the face of a mountain
and the snow was melting—sweet boy—
how high the pitch
and steep the frequency
of your suffering
in my dreams you never survive the frost
but in death walk slowly along the gravel
of a slender winding road
up the side of the sierra
though weightless the earth shifts
beneath your feet
in acknowledgment of your matter
of how you make the ground holy—
hosanna sweet boy hosanna—
you are ascending the mountain
the jet of your skin iridescent
beneath the sun's heat your eyes
turned upwards to count the veins
in the tree leaves the birds in their nests
the beetles black and buzzing

through the branches
along the path flowers lift their faces
in greeting and you joke with them like sisters
full   sated   lush—
at the bend in the road you look down
the cliffside to the space
where the van would be
you don't stop to look for brake marks
or signs of struggle
there are no surprises here
no uncertainty of what this was
only what was and in death is
no longer
you descend through the brush
and collect the bones
of your siblings
gather them like an artist
a benevolent god—all praises—
you lay out their skeletons
joining the joints with daisies
so enamored with your work
you don't notice them
when they come
your brothers and sisters
soundless through mulch
their spirits all glimmer and shine
though a canopy overhead
you grasp each other's hands
and without want or shadow
you meander slowly
toward eden

HERBERT VON KING DOG RUN

high summer and the grass is so green and overgrown
I almost can't see the boy who haunts the run rolling
feral as any loose pup in the dirt
the boy is alone and when we speak
he curses the couples on the lawn
the *Karens* who scold him for being rough
rowdy and careless with their dogs
his hair falls to his shoulders like a basketball net
and sways with every accented *fucking fuck*
he is thirteen and gangly and white
and able to be a child wandering barefaced
into my bubble in the middle of a pandemic
I say *where's your mask?* and he puts it on   *you happy now?*
I smile at his sass and worry he doesn't look cared for
outside the park three officers in plain clothes wait at a bus stop
rules say *you must have a dog to enter*
but no one will cast out this wild child
here he's free

JOURNAL ENTRY:

"HE MADE ME FEEL LIKE A DRUG ADDICT"
—Dr. Susan Moore, who died of COVID-19 after complaining that her symptoms were not being taken seriously by white medical staff.

when he went in to have the cancer cut from his liver Pa was so afraid of the nurses and what they might do to his Black body Mo had to sleep on the small cot beside his bed all three nights while they waited to see how he'd do with the invasion.

I was in high school and he had spent all summer before the surgery saying how glad he'd be for a break from Molly. and when he couldn't bear the idea of being alone with his gaping wound in that white space. I told myself after all this time he was still a boy from the backwoods of mississippi who'd never seen a reason to trust a white man in his life.

I can't understand why white women are so willing to leave their children with strangers. I was babysitting once and a woman I'd only just met handed me her sobbing toddler and walked away. I wanted to cry too. When I was a kid my aunt complained about the nice white teacher who loved her daughter too much. *I swear she's gone run off with my baby* she'd say.

no one ever wants to talk about how close we are to the legacy of enslavement but it's right there. you just choose not to look.

even in a viral pandemic that destroys the lungs the error rate for oximeters is three times higher for dark-skinned patients. a product of whites only studies. a flaw discovered fifteen years ago that no one cares to fix.

10

I've decided I can't trust anyone who uses darkness as a metaphor for what they fear.

on my way into the hospital when I was singing about my rape and begging and begging to go home the man in charge of the ward looked at me like a thing to be got under control. and I knew then I had been outside my mind to go there in my need and think anyone might help me.

ANOTHER BLACK ELDER FINDS ME
WEEPING ON THE SUBWAY

grabs my wrist before exiting the car
who knows what it is about the screeching
moans of the track and all the bodies
pressing in that opens me but it does
and I weep openly into this woman
she is only inches from my face whispering
so I can feel her breathe me in and out
her voice a tether demanding I remain
whatever it is god's got it she says
shaking me like a tambourine before an altar
as if to summon me back into my body
as if she knows how far I've gone

DEAR GABRIEL FERNANDEZ

The fear of the lord is the beginning of knowledge —*Proverbs 1:7*

often I picture your beginning   the mother's blood
washed from your skin with care   the whole of your body
wrinkled and papersoft placed into the arms of the woman
who brought you here and took you out
what she must've seen in your eyes then
the same ones she smeared
with foundation to mask *the fear*
of the lord she beat into your skin   *the blue*
of the wound gifted to cleanse away evil
how to bear them now staring out into the camera—
your veiled ache climbing through
your spirit bound again to the violences
born by flesh—is this what she wanted
a sweet dead boy over a blossoming sissy
dear godless angel   fairy child and waif
I come here with nothing to offer
but your name on my lips   a prayer to the edge
of wordlessness   a curse for the wickedness of god

I'm Tired of Living on an Island, but the Current's Too Heavy to Swim Out

the last person who held me raped me
—story of my life—when I dream of her
we're still together and it's all I think about
the dreams are unpleasant but hardly nightmares
once we were looking at a new apartment
some place in the country I've never been
and there was nothing but green outside and sun coming in
and the living room was so wide and open
and the woman who lived downstairs was offering it to us
at just the right price
and my ex was smiling her *we could be happy here* smile
and I was fine but didn't know what to do
about the stone tumbling down into the basement
or in another we're living
in my father's childhood home for some reason
and it's time for bed
and we're going to sleep where my father's parents slept
where I had slept some nights between them as a girl
unsure of where to put my body
and I'm not a girl in the dream but still so unsure
and the headboard looks exactly as it did
when I was young

"Sometimes I Feel Like I'm Almost Gone"

in the sixth month after your body refused
to keep his secrets   you remember him

home alone with his heart disease his old age
and wonder how long he will sit

slack and sunken before he is found
you picture his body   the ashen cold of his skin

the smell of shit and decay   a mouse
scampering up the arm of the chair to bite

at his eyebrows   you want this
to feel good you say *if there is a god*

then this is how it will happen
you say *god owes me*

if you believed in peace
you'd know this is not the way

but since you have given up believing—

"His Powerful Hand"

no never being an option
your grandmother teaches you
to turn your cheek to keep
the old church mothers
from kissing you dead
on the lips   to wait
to wipe the spittle
and lipstick from your skin
to breathe so shallow
that when the deacon whispers
in your face you don't smell
the sour coffee he tried to hide
with the mint dissolving under his tongue
to sing

I'm coming up   on the rough side
of the mountain   I must hold to god

As Passed from Auntie to Auntie to You

when she names your grandfather
they crowd her little girl body
and convince her of what it mustn't know
they say she doesn't understand
and what grown man and turn
their noses in displeasure
at the child's unbridled tongue
your grandfather is young then
still part of the familial body
testing the heft and shadow
of his deacon's suit
and she is just a small thing
with crisp ribbon binding the braids in her hair
white stockings her mother bleaches clean
for sunday school and the shine of snot
that coats the lips of young children

VOCABULARY LESSON

1. *Pachyderm*

is a mammal with a tough outer skin that is bumpy
a rhino a hippo an elephant

each an object with the same container
but different meanings

you always loved a word
can imagine he must've seen how it delighted you

as you rubbed the leather of his chair
and tried to imagine how a hippo might feel

now you're sure he was checking something
like if you could tell yet

the similarities and differences
in a container

like if you knew when to speak
and when to keep your mouth shut

2. *Nigger*

he gives you a word
the word is nigger
the word means
don't repeat this to your mother

you are young
so young you scarcely a girl
you say the word
perhaps you croon it

as he taught you

when no one was looking

only your mother hears
hears it roll past your lips
hears the bad
she says
it's bad
says don't say that
and you learn
to hold
the bad word
squeeze it like a warhead
burning sour
on your tongue

3. *Grandpa*

there are three bobbys in my family
bobby my father
bobby my brother
and him

I avoid naming as if the claim
would call him in the room again
treat denial like a matter of safety

you try not to but think of the bobbys like pachyderms
better know for sure which is which

who has the horn and who doesn't

I don't call my brother by his first name
only brother brother
keep your kids safe

I stopped saying daddy
and gave up thinking anyone
could keep us safe

"Say It Wasn't My Fault You Suffered"
after Toi Derricotte

head anchored between your hip bones
nudging the cervix from the inside

days the long and weary task of opening
and me all too big from the start

mother   in another era I would've killed
us both   must I alone be blamed

I know the crease of the scar creeping up
your belly   how after my brothers were pulled

limb by limb from that same crater
you cradled the wound so gingerly

I worried you might split apart
mother you don't have to forgive me

I know what it's like to refuse
and still be opened

II.

ENTHUSIASTIC CONSENT

no matter how you've been lonely
in bed together you think you need her here

breathing and restless beside you
she who won't listen or repeat the phrase

enthusiastic consent
without smirking *how do you measure that?*

you measure loneliness by the places you linger
the people you let close to you

tonight she won't be stayed
won't be settled or held close

like the others   she rises above you
kneels like them too   opens your legs or tries to

and you haven't spoken for hours
hadn't planned to till morning

you squeeze your legs
and push her arms away
you grow frantic

and she likes it
your enthusiasm

you try not to recognize the dance
take and take

you think   she can't be stronger than me
you push back harder

but she won't give up

she pulls your legs
you push her hands away

your body animal and mute with sleeplessness
her hands and your hands and the squeeze of
your thighs fighting for possession

oh sweet silent object
oh unwilling and desperate body

you are losing you are losing you aren't fighting anymore

I'm Tired of Living on an Island, but the Current's Too Heavy to Swim Out

daphne was determined
to die for the longest
she would just rain
dry yellow needles
all over the desk
till I nearly expected
a sprout to spring
from the mulch
so I moved her
to the ledge
where the sun's brightest
near plant baby
who I love most
because she was first
and never minded
a little neglect
though she can be dramatic as hell
with her branches
and leaves drooping
like some sad
little willow
when she's been too long without
sable I found
in the garbage
and she's been content
with whatever spot
she's gotten inside
ever since
each morning
when jerome opens
to greet the sun
I imagine
he whispers

hallelujah
and every night
when he closes
amen
willie earl
I named for my uncle
who died
the wise old
elephant ears
open
so lusciously
green

I'm Tired of Living on an Island, but the Current's Too Heavy To Swim Out

my therapist wants to know how I wound up here
she asks me to describe the island
so I tell her about the well
I spend my time in
it's deep and shaded but not too cold
I like the way my voice talks back to me
bouncing along the corrugated stone
when I'm bored I like to sing and drum
and let the orchestra swell between my ears
my therapist asks if I can get out of the well
if I want out of the well
she doesn't quite get
that it doesn't matter
it's just where I live
one day the wind will chase the water
over the ground and I won't live here anymore
or maybe something else less bleak
either way

HERE
after & for John Allen Taylor

after nine hours on a turnpike lousy with deer—
some almost sleeping   others just a flush
opening and so much blood
these nearly always in drowsy sundown towns
perhaps as a reminder of whose country this is anyway perhaps to say
nigger you better hurry along before the
sun declines to bear witness—
after we're done with family done with holiday cheer
we meet in a bar a few miles from detroit
though it may as well have been new england
for all its white picket fences   kitschy bales
of hay   and oak leaves crimson
as the coasts of the pacific at the close of day
we order beers we muddle through familiarity and distance
how fast are you dying we ask   *how well are you performing wellness*
we forget to be careful *how fresh are the scars*   we forget
to lower our voices *are they healing*   we are like salmon
flopping around the fisherman's boat   reckless   desperate
sometimes slowly you say *sometimes not at all* I say *too often too fast*
we glance at the flat screens mounted in the corners like bucks' heads
another #MeToo muted   another reminder of all we are lo   sing
of what we never had to begin with
the light of it playing across our faces   the world
a steady bleakening   a clotted scream
the other day my therapist asked if she ought to be concerned for me
and I heard *do I need to take you from yourself*
you tell me how you were taken once   how you only just
convinced them to give you back   I tell you what keeps me here
we both pretend it is enough
I could tell you how afraid I am   but with our
knees knocking below the counter
like siblings like we are simply trying to
be sure of ourselves to be sure

we are both here   both solid tender flesh
I could tell you how afraid I am but we
are too much like trees I think
each of us sending the other sugar through the roots
though we are both sick   I say I'd miss your poems
you say to call when I feel like leaving   we hug we part
each of us down our own lonely road
my dearest brother I promise I'll stay here
promise you will too

LOVE POEM TO THE MOTHERFUCKER
WHO BROKE INTO MY APARTMENT

all I'm saying is that was some good ass weed you stole
top shelf and you better have enjoyed it

I mean you looked like you needed some flower
the way you clutched the tin against your chest and leapt

down the stairs   ok I didn't really see you leap
I was running for my life too after all

me out the front door you through the basement
the man who chased you down the street for no other reason

than the frantic in me could've been my brother
but you could've been my brother too

frozen a split second exiting my bedroom door
as if you were the doe

and not the semi barreling towards me
I didn't want to call the cops on you

but you had my laptop too and had been inside my bedroom
and I have been the doe my whole life and it frightened me

they say you ditched my laptop when you started hopping fences
the sirens howling in broad daylight pumping cortisol

and adrenaline into your thighs and heart   run
run run run   forgive me

I wanted you far from me   yes
but also I want you alive and free

Poem Where My Dog Is the Hero

sleeping my dog Lili likes to nestle
between my legs
high up by the thighs
my one leg arching over
like a bridge she runs to for shelter
butt to butt
nose to calf
we slumber
and she keeps my pussy from danger
sometimes I tell jokes about her clinginess
pretending to be annoyed
with how she claims the center of my bed
in my dreams though she's always there
lips curled up exposing her teeth
setting a boundary like she does when another dog
won't heed her subtler cues or acting how she gets
when the wrong men get too close
too interested after dark
when my ex kneels to force
her hand inside me
Lili releases a low grumbling growl
try it and I'll take your fingers
and I drift quietly back into sleep
peaceful and not raped

LOVE POEM

all night you get up to check on the baby
your little niece swaddled
like a perfect burrito
breathing so softly
you worry her lungs will stop if you sleep
in the morning   red eyed and cloudy
you hand the baby to your mother
and she laughs at your worry
says she's restless when she keeps O too
though she never felt that way with you all
maybe because you were mine
you imagine her then
baby-faced in the hospital
delirious from drugs and labor
a newborn on her chest
screaming and screaming unable to latch
and your mother the youngest of seven
who never cared for anything in her life
somehow supposed to make it better

Sometimes You Can Stare and Stare at a Thing and Never See What It Is

I hate rats
they remind me of something

I can't or won't place
the city is full of rats

I don't walk after sundown to avoid them
I stomp my feet down dark alleys
so they have time to scamper away

mostly I put them
so far outside my mind

I forget
they exist

until I see one darting
from a trash pile

my friend has to say *rat trap!*
before I see

the black boxes littered
all over brooklyn

sometimes it's trickier
like with the rat I couldn't avoid

on the walk from the train in boston
so I named him Ralph

and said *hello Ralph*

every night on my walk home
one day Ralph got smashed by a tire

something tasty in the road and he forgot to run
I couldn't bring myself
to look closely at the remains

but remember
how shocked I was to see

the other rat puttering
around his body

how I had only made peace
with the solitary rodent

and not the dense inevitable infestation

My Mother Reads Her Bible

after the minister has read the scripture
and began to preach a good word
my mother circles back to the head
and carries on past
the pastor's delicately plucked verse
packed in the Los Angeles warehouse we called sanctuary
where we praised god so loud you could find your way to the altar
through the haze of the baldfaced factory buildings
blending one into the other
on the other side of the unused rail tracks
sure as the elders could find their way to the prayer meetings
hidden way back in the woods of mississippi
from the sounds of the *yes lords*
rising to kiss the tree leaves alone
my mother a martin luther
among the caught up masses
trusted no one
least of all a man
who would have himself
anointed above her

and I had trusted
my mother
had seen how she could fight
the teachers who didn't think
we were smart enough
white enough
had seen her read a man for filth
had heard her say she was too crazy
for anyone to touch her daughter
had seen her smile
at the man who hurt me
and believe him
when he said it wasn't my fault

and though he hadn't been talking about me
I had never seen my mother
be wrong
and so when she believed him
I did too
even above myself

"What Cannot Be Communicated to the Mother Cannot Be Communicated to the Self"

—John Bowlby, expert in Attachment Theory,
Cognitive Behavioral Theory

she shows her mother the stain
filling the gusset of her panties
like an inkblot test
and the mother names it *fine*
so the girl learns to be *fine*
and doesn't think of it
not even years after
when her breasts swell
like mosquito bites and she learns
like other girls to rinse out blood
in cold water rubbing the fabric
between her knuckles
until her fingers grow stiff as ice

~

children don't get weary
children don't get weary
children don't get weary
till your work is done

~

but I'm tired
momma I'm so
tired I'm so mom
ma i'm so but i'm so
so tired i'm so tired
momma i'm so
i'm so i
'm so

so
so
so

Pendulum
after Keith Wilson

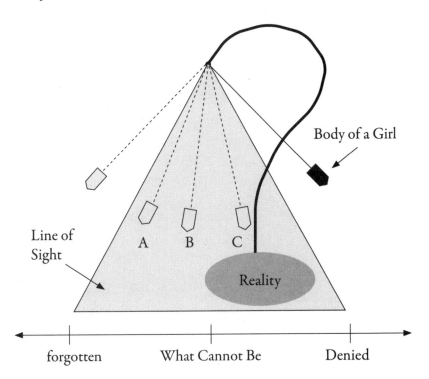

Line of Sight

Body of a Girl

A B C

Reality

forgotten   What Cannot Be   Denied

Key

A) the sense of someone else in the room and then the weight: dense and immobile: a wall of brick on her chest
B) on an elevated surface: the surface is contextual if you saw a scalpel you'd call it an operating table: (you must not call it a bed)
C) chewing pork someone has coated and fried with oil: taste of sandpaper and ash: the girl's jaw moving slower and slower: the flesh a solid lump greeting the bile at her throat

Before

it was summer and so hot
you couldn't tell the sweat

from the pool water
gathering in fat droplets

on our sunbrowned skin
one of them days

me and my cousins
was so free

so cute
you couldn't tell us shit

granny had let us walk to rite aid
to buy candy with the few dollars

she could spare for our sugar high
she would drive past

on our route
just to be sure

we was still alive

when we got back home
we flew upstairs real quick

so we wouldn't have to share with our brothers
so granny wouldn't see

the bubblegum
my momma said would rot my teeth

my back had been hurting all the way home
but it hadn't mattered

cause I was wearing this three quarter swimsuit top
with a little midriff showing

and these real cute white shorts
K saw the blood first

and screamed like she thought
I was dying

she was two years younger than me
and I was young to be bleeding

so she probably thought I really was dying
we had been changing

in a rush to get back to the pool
and I had thrown those white shorts

upside down on the bed
and there it was pooling

like a stripe on somebody's flag

and what about the time before?
the first time
there was blood?

what about it?

what happened before?

I had come home

from somewhere.

where?

I don't know.

A███████MEN█

you do not understand ████████████████

████████████████████████

████████████████████████████

████████████████████████████

████████████████████████████

██████████████ memory ████████████████

████████████████████████████

█████ the origin of █████ fear █████

████████████████████████████

█████████████████████ the passing,

████████████████████████████

████████████████████████████

████████████████████ whisper

████████████████████ slick with sweat

all those ████ years. ████████████learning

the tip- toed walk ████████████████████

████████████████████████████

██████████████████ you know

he must have ████████ but you cannot███

████████████████████████████

████████████████████████████

█ hear ████████████████████████

████████ it ████ too present

████████████████████████████

████████████████████

████████████████████, the faint scent of terror, ████████

43

                will

his will.
you feel   his body
      choke on   his

      hard love

      you say

      my sins *. nothing.*
~
but *blood*

      still

    you fear
      salvation,
      tremble

beneath the feet of saints.
    allowed   forget—

      the bruised
  fracture

      to hide
      memory

in the lines ██████████████████████

████████████████████████████
of their hands ██████████

RESURRECTION

nasal swab stretching your nose   the no
where to run of it   the entering   and there you are again

trembling barrettes on your pigtails   *no no no*
rammed back down your throat   the shut eyes   the familial
inevitable   the refusal to witness

you can hear the doctor trying to count you through
the invasion   but she is so far and too late now anyway

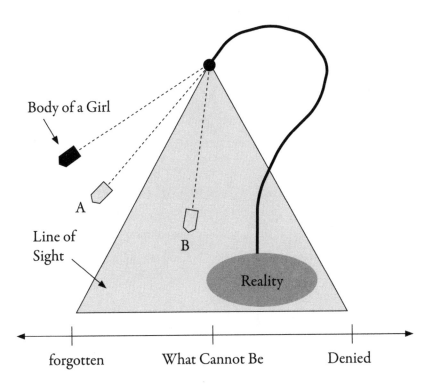

A)   base maybe but never the head   normal thickness   hair curl-
ing like tar covered springs like tires from all the wrecks   a sea of
swirling spirals   of snakes deadly and clambering for the neck—my
neck—the skin beneath peaking through—his skin—a desert sand
you're sure it'd burn to touch

B)   he's all over me
      and he's keeping me alive
      he's all over me
      and he's keeping me alive.

III.

Self-Portrait with My Parents' Wedding Anniversary

only a few times did your mother have love enough
to ignore the rot and venom of her disgust
for your father   the man she kept like a noose
at her neck so you and your brothers
wouldn't be another number
in the graphics fox news makes denouncing Black
fatherless children going nowhere but prison fast
then she'd nod a halfhearted assent and they'd pack
for vegas and your father would call up his dad
who despite his sister's sweat soaked fear he would not give up
then it was north up the 605
north toward the San Gabriel Mountains
knotty with brush and ruinous with fire
hell's inferno come up to fill the sky with ash
this normal as your grandfather ready and waiting
in his normal house with the normal neighbors
who don't know to listen or look
for the noiseless way a girl is ground down
to nothing and no one   her spirit a sightless nomad
wandering the dusty knolls at the base of the mountain
her body a no man's land waiting for her
mother and father to return

SELF-PORTRAIT WITH A LINE FROM AN OLD HYMN

". . . and there may I though vile as he. . . " from "There is a Fountain"

and how thick a stain
how deep
through how many layers
how sunken in the flesh
through skin and fat and muscle
viscera bone
to the marrow even
I'm too scared to look
can you see it
smell it
evidence it
getitoffmegetitoffmegetitoffmegetitoffmegetitoffmegetitoffmegetitoffme
on facebook a man wants to know
fellas if your wife gets raped by ____ men
you sticking with her
or is that something you can't get passed
can't bear to taste
can taste
can you taste it
going rancid
sharp and acrid
how acidic
I think I feel it sometimes
can you see it burning
is it burning
am I burning
and tell me where shall I
how shall I
wash oh wash wash wash wash wash
and what blood
with whose blood
whose blood
whose blood

getitoffmegetitoffmegetitoffmegetitoffmegetitoffmegetitoffmegetitoffme
and whose sins
who wash oh wash oh wash wash wash
wash wash wash wash wash wash
away

When Spite Is the Only Thing That Feeds You

bite down and break the skin against your teeth
chew
take full possession of your mouth
let it hang open
or purse the lips tight as a zipper
so not a morsel
slips loose
stay present
and if the past comes knocking
your grandfather's hands
popping up all over your body
bite down again
harder
use all of your teeth
the canines the incisors
grind the flesh down
between your molars
until it's a mushy lump at your throat
swallow
swallow again
keep what you can down
and what you can't spit into the air
be a child again
wipe the grease from your lips like blood
and rub the residue into your jeans
laugh
let it be hysterical

Dear Mother I'm Angry

dear mother I hold my anger like a grappling hook
dear mother my anger wears me like a glove
dear mother wait for me
dear mother I worry my anger will outlast me
dear mother I am gripping my anger by
the throat like a strangled hen
dear mother I have strangled my anger
dear mother do you want to know what it takes to strangle
dear mother I have buried my anger on the side
of the road like an accident victim
dear mother nothing rises with the dead like anger
dear mother sometimes the anger flows
through me like the breath of life
dear mother no matter what I do all I breathe is fire
dear mother it burns
dear mother I have found the fire extinguisher
and hit my anger over the head with it
dear mother I fear sometimes the anger is madness
dear mother my anger is still here nestled beside me like a stray dog

Sometimes When I Grumble

I sound like my grandfather
who raped me
and it's always surprising
his groans rumbling up
like magma to scorch the earth
when I'm vulnerable
or in pain
you'd forgive me for wanting
to cut off the source
put a stopper in it
a plug a gag a pacifier
I swear it's a full-time job
soothing my inner child
neediest whimpering thing
and I don't know what to tell her
when he comes wheezing from our throat
it's not my fault
though still I find myself on my knees
before the bleary-eyed child
begging please forgive me
forgive me forgive me

Love Poem to Brionne at Sunset

what would you have me do with your rage
how many fires shall I start
how many times shall we tear ourselves open
what are you dragging me back to
I don't want to go love
I don't want to go
don't make me
I know
I'm a terrible witness
I'm sorry
but let's not
not tonight
I'll give you your bonfire
if you let me turn memory to ash
let's live like fireflies
I promise you
they exist
we exist
you exist
let's live only from one flash of light to the next
let's own the night
let's stone fear
let's not look any further
let's not look back
just close your eyes love
release your fists
you are here now
and it is safe
you are safe here
I promise you
you're ok

Every Poem I Write I Ask Permission

to exist   I keep the history of my body
locked away in a file labeled *do not name*

more often than not I'm grieving
which is why doves peek in
at my window

every morning
I thank god

for how my family
could always laugh after funerals

I am estranged

from god and have this terrible belief
if I found the right words

she would understand
and say *oh my dear my dear*

it's true I'm talking about my mother again

and true as well I've made the decisions for you
but I can't bear it!

this tremble and waiting
to see when or if or how you might love me

LOVE POEM

it takes too long to realize you don't know how to fight
years you treasured the memories of play fighting
with your brother   the animal joy at being bigger
stronger by almost three years replaced with the dance
of learning to box with someone who's got
four inches on your wingspan
then you'd tuck your torso into a ball and ram your body into his
feather punching his gut until the drama of his retreat
or the bear grip of his arms hauling you into air
like your father when you were a girl
and still thought daddy was the strongest man you knew
now you watch your brother place his daughter gingerly
into the bassinet for a little *independent woman time*
and think of how she too will learn to spar with her father
and if she's lucky never realize it's only dance

ANDROGYNY

you can remember
how it stretched
the width
of your shoulders
broad like your brothers
how you never wanted
to be him   boy child
namesake of the father
who called you babygirl
made sure you could dribble
with your right
and left hands
read a madden playbook
pull worms from a bait box
without squealing
you think you can remember
the day your parents
brought your brother home
how when your mother
pushed her tapered nipple
into his infant mouth
you pressed your baby
hard and plastic
against your flat
chest and fostered life too
at times you thought
it was only about power
how you didn't want
to give up the feeling
of wrestling
your forearm circled
about your brother's neck
his head locked
his hips pinned

by your legs
the smug feeling of mercy
on his lips before letting go
you can admit
you envied him
how one day
he would grow tall
mighty as your father
while your body
would only soften and bleed
how when he caught
the pigskin your father
let fly through air
he was only good
as he should be
how when he sent
the ball back
spiral tight as a drill
through bone
he was only throwing
like himself

My Mother Wants to Know I'll Still Be a Bride

on my wedding day
none of this wanting
to be a man like those other queers

my mother has always dreamt of me
in a bustle of tulle and lace
a train trailing all the way down the aisle

only I can make her mother of the bride

no matter how many dress fittings
hair cake and catering appointments
she attends with my cousins

I couldn't tell you what a man is

but I've tried and don't fit
neatly into the other box
there's always my knee
or shoulder poking out

lately I'm tired of being hemmed in

and can't help but imagine
there must be other options

like how my mother would pull out her camera
and put my brothers into my old flowered dress

just to see what they'd look like if they were girls

how she always told them how pretty they looked
how I knew that I was them
a boy twirling in his dress

Tuning

to annoy me sitting in traffic
on random take your niece to work days
my uncle liked to sing off-key
while I'd beg him to shut up
or find his way to a chord
he always knew
how to press on people's buttons
knew I had a good ear
but not as good an ear
as I believed
sing in your own key
and I'll stop he'd say
harmony had always been easy for me
and I was too young then
to see the purpose of discord
the radio pushed out the tune
and I followed the progressions
whether I wanted to or not
watching me struggle to break loose from the chord
my uncle said *you have to hear*
the people sing and yourself
you have to hear yourself louder

I Like to Wear My Mother's Clothes

I underpack when I go home
leave a little room

for the sweatpants
ballooning kneelength shorts
the black and white striped maxi dress

I'll ferry back and wear like a time traveler
lost in an aggressively gentrified brooklyn

my mother shops when she's sad
not that she'd say she was sad
just struggling with where to put everything

we've both got a thing about clutter
something we're trying to fill or stock up against

once I walked into a room
and she said *I had a pair of green shorts just like those*
and I said *I know these them*

my mother wants a mini me and says so
all her sisters have one
even the cousins too

when I was twelve I climbed five inches over my mother
but didn't outgrow her dainty size seven feet

she'd leave her sandals by the door
and I would slide into them running outside
to help bring in groceries or just play horse with my brother

when I was younger my mother loved to
dress she and I in matching outfits

green shirts and blue jeans for st patrick's day
matching track suits in red and purple for valentine's day

brand new christmas pajamas every year
I knew my mother loved me the year she agreed
to the powder blue pajamas she hated
with "Let It Snow" in bold letters on the shirt front

In Search of a New God

Scripture: ~~Honor thy father and mother and~~
~~your days will be long on this earth~~

Revision: Get free and when you do take all who are willing to walk

Praxis:
try not to leave your mother
even when her eyes move like scalpels looking for the parts of you
she'd shave away cut off like a wart she's grown tired of looking at
instead watch the way she bites her tongue
and try not to fill in what she might say
if she wasn't trying to respect your boundaries
remember you are teaching new vocabulary
new ways of moving of shaking off that *old rugged cross*
remember you both spring from the same root
and how love has tangled your freedom all up in with hers
and remember Harriet hunched over in the
painting at your auntie's house
her rifle pointing towards the sky her hand reaching firmly back
to protect the ones she ferried   say *get behind me mother*
and don't forget the rifle points both ways
and no matter how the dogs press and the nights screech with horror
turning back was never an option

Let's Pretend My Mother Says "I'm Sorry"

you were so helpless and new and I had held
my sisters' babies when they were born
but never been left alone to nurture
something so small and barely formed
and I had struggled just to get you here
had gone toe to toe with death alone
negotiated for our survival and let blood
so you could live   it didn't matter if I wanted to give
when your father bent to suck and see if he couldn't pull
something out   there was no milk   and I had labored
damn near three days just to get to you
and *here you were screaming* like it was my fault
and that's how it went   no matter what I did
you made me feel small and not enough
and I knew no way around fault
so I gifted it all to you

JOSHUA TREE

after I saw my dragon napping in the gossamer clouds
I danced swaying like a palm through warm september gales
R witness to the music my feet made dragging
across linoleum   outside the desert grows loud
with nightcrawlers and the mountain covers her face
as I howl my pleasure at the nibbled moon
I watch my body move in the windows black void
and fall in love with the wild and coil the shimmy and tender
our mothers didn't get to do this R says
shrooms I say *this* she says
exhaling a fog of smoke with a pleased grin
lips pursed I decide that like my mother I look beautiful when I pout
I have time   thank god   and am learning
to love myself from the outside in
she'd hate this but I wish I could bring her here
quietly I invite my mother in and sit her down at the table
I tell her what I can't say
and it doesn't matter whether she hears me

My Mother Fights for Every Last Dime of Her Mother's Refund

this has nothing to do with the value of a dollar
or anything anybody might need
the sales associate is simply mistaken
she thinks she can outlast my mother
but doesn't know how long the ledgers been stacked against us
my mother's mother the daughter of sharecroppers
her ugly middle name a bartering chip
a soiled hammy down from the white lady
whose land they sucked a living from
as if after all her mother's lonely labor   even this
even the child who came wrinkled and slick
with her own blood wasn't hers in the end
Jardine   Mo's lips curl like the taste
of rotting flesh on the tongue just to say it
don't you give that name to any of your children she says
flaring her nose   a wide line drawn be-
tween miss'ssippi and california
as if that was all it took to keep the haints behind us
on the call the associate is trying to convince my mother
she doesn't know how to read
the charges spread out like a field of black ink
as if my mother had been the one
crammed into a one-room schoolhouse
her books picked apart by the white kids
who owned them before
nigger scribbled on every page
my mother has never bowed her head for anyone
and I know today ain't the day she starts
I can hear the ice in her voice
each word freezing to a dagger's point
hear the *I wish a mother fucker would*
in each crisp enunciated syllable
she's been twice as good for half as much

67

and has felt everything the world can take
she has seen her mother feel this too
outside Mo pats the earth
around the birds of paradise in their flower beds
she said she wouldn't spend her life
in someone else's dirt and didn't
above her the birds crane their necks toward the sun
the orange and blue plumes shiny with dew
their beaks green and silent swaying in the breeze
at times it seems they'll fly

LOVE POEM

after I cut mine my mother asks
what I will do when she is too old
to raise her arms above her head
to dust the crop that grows like wild grasses
leaping from her skull this isn't the first
time she's asked how I will care for her
when it's time though it is always
about her hair how I'll probably cut it off
or lock it up how after all this time
and all her skill I never acquired any
of my own then I like to say
I will take her to the hair salon
as if I don't know she is asking
how much and how well I love her
sometimes I say she'd better start teaching
the grandkids how to warm a hot plate
and part the hair evenly at the root
most days though I can already see my gloved hands
slippery with dye and all that stubborn gray at the base
I'll pull the widetooth comb slowly
through the length of her hair
it will almost be enough

GEOMETRY OF LOVE
after Taylor Johnson

if my mother loves me then love hurts

if love hurts then it will not save

if you wanna be saved grandma say you got to call the name of jesus

if you calling on jesus you better have all   three his numbers landline personal and work cellphone

if you call all three a jesus' numbers and he still don't answer then just know the brother was busy

if the brother is busy then you better have someone else to call

if you've got no one else to call then you know what it's like to be alone

in the wilderness beneath a canopy of gawkingstars

if the stars are gawking then you must've crossed over

if you've crossed over then you know what it is to be chased from home

if you've been chased from home was that ever really home to begin with?

if you've never been somewhere that felt like home start with what feels good against your skin

if love feels good against your skin then call it home and don't worry the shape it takes

if the shape of love is liquid and mercurial then call yourself a shapeshifter *lean with it rock with it*

if you a shapeshifter then baby you can be anything you like

if you can be anything you like twist and turn go forward and double back until you find what it is that gives you joy

if you can find what gives you joy then the world is all yours

if the world is yours be generous tear open the bread and share it

70

We've Come This Far by Faith

bullheaded beautiful and black
you be a galaxy
infinite and dusted with stars
lean into the absence
the dark obstinate abyss
be a wormhole
pull everything in
even when your grandmothers
didn't know what to pray for
they still prayed for you
if you believe in nothing
believe in you
sing to the child in the well
sing until she unfurls her fist
until she sings too
get her out
take her with you
straighten your back beloved
nobody was ever promised they'd live

THE BOUNDARY

made of stone maybe   the opal shades of rock
blending like the surface of a pond in watercolor
I'd grow vegetables on my side

my mother would plant roses on hers
when the sun was out   the sky blue and warm
we'd stand with our hoses spraying the ground

trading tips on how to get rid of snails
or keep the weeds from returning in summer

on rainy days my mother would sit in her house
shaking her head at the bleak gray clouds
and I would pull on my raincoat to take out my dog

sometimes a stone would fall when the weather got bad
and after we'd stand crossarmed at the border
muttering about what the other ought to do to fix it

sometimes whole sections would fail
the stones crushing a rose bush or vine of sweet peas

my mother peeking through to turn her nose up at my mess
and my dog jumping over to dig holes in her lawn

we'd get fed up but never move
in spring my mother's fruit trees would blossom
and by summer she'd have avocados putting a bend in the branches

on a good day she'd pass over a bag of stone fruit
and I might hand her a crisp green plume of collards

AGAINST MASTERY

give me no seat at the table
let no trembling hands lay food on my plate

let me lord over no one and nothing
not the dog curled up in my bed

not the land nor children who wander
through my care   let me learn from the babies

and be always laughing at my ignorance
only humble discovery   give me

and keep my eyes on the pattern of birds' wings
breaking the blue overhead   let me face

the ones I harm with open palms and let love
be the method and measure of my worth

keep my heart with my people
and the coal glowing beneath my feet

let me run and run and run and run
and let the flame of my torch never go out

I am here with you
to burn the house down

keep me to this   cut me down
before you let me lose my way

NOTES

"Want and Love Are Not the Same Word" is a quote taken from Nicole Homer's poem "The Overlap," which can be found in her book *Pecking Order*.

"Journal Entry: 'he made me feel like a drug addict'" is how Dr. Susan Moore, a Black doctor who died of complications from COVID-19, described being mistreated by her attending physician.

"Sometimes I Feel Like I'm Almost Gone" is a line borrowed from the spiritual "Sometimes I Feel Like a Motherless Child."

The title "His Powerful Hand" and the lines "I'm coming up / on the rough side of the mountain / I must hold to god" are borrowed from the gospel song "Rough Side of the Mountain."

"Say It Wasn't My Fault You Suffered" is a line from Toi Derricotte's poem "Another poem of a small grieving for my fish Telly," which can be found in her book *The Undertaker's Daughter*.

"What Cannot Be Communicated to the Mother Cannot Be Communicated to the Self" takes its title and concept from psychologist John Bowlby, who studied Attachment Theory and Cognitive Behavioral Theory.

"A▆▆men▆" is an erasure of my poem "Atonement" in my second book, *Blessed are the Peacemakers*.

"He's all over me / and he's keeping me alive" is a lyric from the song "He's All Over Me" by Whitney Houston.

"Honor thy father and mother and your days will be long on this earth" is a line paraphrased from the Bible verse Exodus 20:12.

Acknowledgments

American Poetry Review: "Against Mastery," "For Devonte Hart"

Diode: "As Passed from Auntie to Auntie to You," "When Spite Is the Only Thing That Feeds You"

Rosebud Magazine: "Here"

The Rumpus:"Journal Entry: he made me feel like a drug addict," "Say It Wasn't My Fault You Suffered"

The VIDA Review: "My Mother Fights for Every Last Dime of Her Mother's Refund"

West Trestle Review: "Every Poem I Write I Ask Permission"

Rock and Sling Magazine: "Dear Gabriel Fernandez"

About the Author

Brionne Janae is a poet and teaching artist living in Brooklyn. They are the author of *Blessed are the Peacemakers* (2021), winner of the 2020 Cave Canem Northwestern University Press Poetry Prize, and *After Jubilee* (2017), published by Boat Press. Brionne is a 2023 NEA Creative Writing Fellow, a Hedgebrook Alum and proud Cave Canem Fellow. Their poetry has been published in *Best American Poetry 2022*, *Ploughshares*, *The American Poetry Review*, The Academy of American Poet's "Poem-a-Day" series, *The Sun Magazine*, *jubilat*, and *Waxwing* among others. Brionne is the co-host of the podcast *The Slave Is Gone*, alongside poet Jericho Brown and Rogue Scholar, Aife Murray. Off the page they go by "Breezy."

About Haymarket Books

Haymarket Books is a radical, independent, nonprofit book publisher based in Chicago. Our mission is to publish books that contribute to struggles for social and economic justice. We strive to make our books a vibrant and organic part of social movements and the education and development of a critical, engaged, and internationalist Left.

We take inspiration and courage from our namesakes, the Haymarket Martyrs, who gave their lives fighting for a better world. Their 1886 struggle for the eight-hour day—which gave us May Day, the international workers' holiday—reminds workers around the world that ordinary people can organize and struggle for their own liberation. These struggles—against oppression, exploitation, environmental devastation, and war—continue today across the globe.

Since our founding in 2001, Haymarket has published more than nine hundred titles. Radically independent, we seek to drive a wedge into the risk-averse world of corporate book publishing. Our authors include Angela Y. Davis, Arundhati Roy, Keeanga-Yamahtta Taylor, Eve L. Ewing, aja monet, Mariame Kaba, Naomi Klein, Rebecca Solnit, Olúfẹ́mi O. Táíwò, Mohammed El-Kurd, José Olivarez, Noam Chomsky, Winona LaDuke, Robyn Maynard, Leanne Betasamosake Simpson, Howard Zinn, Mike Davis, Marc Lamont Hill, Dave Zirin, Astra Taylor, and Amy Goodman, among many other leading writers of our time. We are also the trade publishers of the acclaimed Historical Materialism Book Series.

Haymarket also manages a vibrant community organizing and event space in Chicago, Haymarket House, the popular Haymarket Books Live event series and podcast, and the annual Socialism Conference.

Also Available from Haymarket Books

All the Blood Involved in Love, Maya Marshall

Black Queer Hoe, Britteney Black Rose Kapri

The BreakBeat Poets Vol. 2: Black Girl Magic, ed. by Mahogany L. Browne, Idrissa Simmonds, and Jamila Woods

Build Yourself a Boat, Camonghne Felix

Can I Kick It?, Idris Goodwin

Citizen Illegal, José Olivarez

I Remember Death by Its Proximity to What I Love, Mahogany L. Browne

Lineage of Rain, Janel Pineda

Mama Phife Represents, Cheryl Boyce-Taylor

Milagro, Penelope Allegria

The Patron Saint of Making Curfew, Tim Stafford

Rifqa, Mohammed El-Kurd

Super Sad Black Girl, Diamond Sharp

There Are Trans People Here, H. Melt

Too Much Midnight, Krista Franklin